This pharmacy adventure belongs to

....

ISBN - 978-1-7635646-1-9

First published in 2024

For Rena, who inspired me to create this book. RL

For Jun Ni, who unleashed the little illustrator's dream within me. PJN

For my sister, Jun Ni who believes in education and sharing knowledge. JMH

"Ana caught a cold yesterday" says Luca.

"Oh no!" cries Maya.
"Let's ask Aunty Sophie for help.

She is a PHARMACIST."

Pronounce

FAAR-muh-sist

2

"What is a **PHARMACIST**?"
Luca wonders.

3

"Pharmacists take care of your health. We give people the right medicine when they really need it." Aunty Sophie explains.

PHARMACY

4

"What is a MEDICINE?" Maya asks.

Pronounce –
MEH-di-sen

5

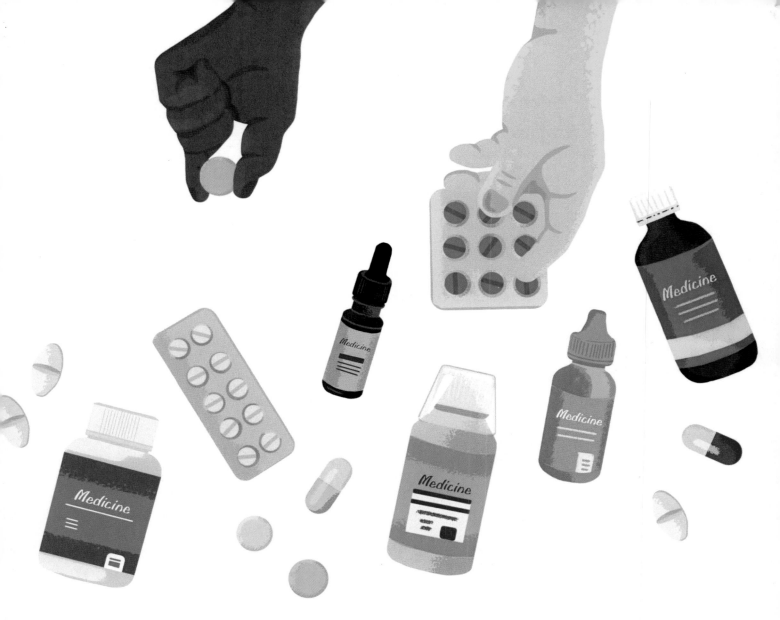

"Made with different ingredients, like a special mix,
Medicines help you get better when you feel sick."

6

"Oh! So can I take a medicine whenever I feel sick?" asks Maya.

"Very often you can get better on your own, with lots of rest, fluids and loving cuddles,

Other times medicines can help you get better,
so you can splash in muddy puddles."

"Oh, I have had this before when I had a fever!"

Luca exclaims, holding a medicine bottle.

Paracetamol

"Yes, this is called
paracetamol,"
Aunty Sophie nods.

Pronounce

Pa-ruh-SEE-tuh-mol

"This is a medicine that can ease your fever,
Like a cooling rain, or a refreshing shower!"

10

"Oh no. Some medicines are for fever, some for stuffy nose,

Some help with fighting germs, like firemen with a hose."

"My big sister Ana caught a cold yesterday.

Can I give her my medicine at home?" asks Luca.

13

"Unlike Rainbow Fish with his shimmering scales to share,

Your medicine is **only for you**, we need to be aware."

"Ana won't need to take medicines," Aunty Sophie continues.

"She needs a lot of rest and to drink plenty of water."

14

"Okay!" says Luca.

"Actually, I do not know where we store our medicines at home," Luca thinks hard.

"Medicine should be stored **out of your reach and sight.**

Like Jack's beanstalk, up high, that's right."

16

"I really like this one - it says it tastes like orange!" says Maya excitedly.

"Can I drink them all, Aunty Sophie?"

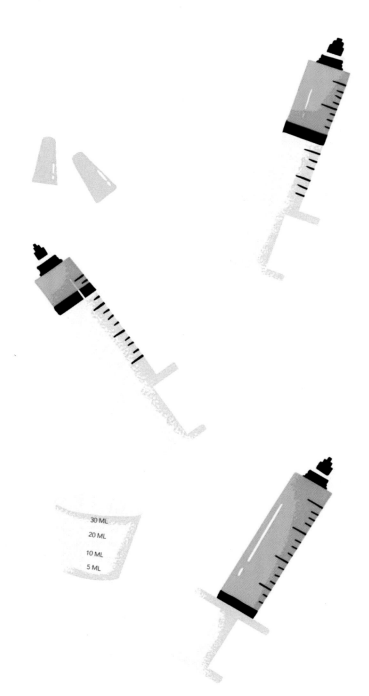

"We need to take the
right amount,
not too little, not too much,

Like Goldilocks finding
porridge with the perfect
gentle touch."

18

"Ugh, I don't like this one.

This smells weird!" says Maya, looking disgusted.

"You can **mix** it with something **sweet**, like honey for Winnie the Pooh,

Remember not to add too much, or we will need to start anew."

19

HONEY

"Luca, let's go check on Ana!" cheers Maya.

Aunty Sophie smiles and continues
"Before you go, I have two other things
to let you know."

"Lollies and medicines, always **ask an adult** before you take, They look very much alike, we should not take medicine by mistake."

TICK

TOCK

23

"Lastly, like Hickory dickory
dock, we'll chime,

We take medicine,
when needed,
at the **right time.**"

TOCK

24

"This is so much fun.
Thank you, Aunty Sophie.

We have learnt so much on our
pharmacy adventure!"

25

26

FIP FOUNDATION
FOR EDUCATION
AND RESEARCH

Royalties from this book will be donated to the
International Pharmaceutical Federation (FIP) Foundation.

The FIP Foundation is a non-for-profit organisation that aims to promote the educational
and research ventures of pharmacists and pharmaceutical scientists and expand the role
of the pharmacist in charitable projects towards better global health.
For more information, visit www.fipfoundation.org

Thank you for supporting our book!
To access free printable resources, such as ABC charts and colouring
sheets, please visit www.pharmacyadventure.com or scan the QR code.

Made in the USA
Las Vegas, NV
04 October 2024

96312768R00019